LOVE
Lasts Forever

A JOURNAL OF MEMORIES

NOELLE K ANDREW & SHEILA B FRASCHT

ISBN: 1483994554
ISBN-13: 9781483994550

LOVE
Lasts Forever

Noelle K Andrew, MDiv, BCC
Sheila B Frascht RN, CHPPN, CT
Illustrations by Nina Scott

"A wife who loses a husband is called a widow. A husband who loses a wife is called a widower. A child who loses his parents is called an orphan. But...there is no word for a parent who loses a child; that's how awful the loss is."

Neugeboren, 1976

Dedication page

"Love Lasts Forever" is a journal for parents and families who have endured the death of a child. It offers the space to reflect on your child's life, to preserve special memories, and to find healing and comfort.

This book is dedicated to those children and families at University of Iowa Children's Hospital who have displayed such grace and strength during times of fear, darkness, and loss. From you, we have learned so much about life's blessings and the power of love.

In Loving Memory

In Memory of: _____

Date of Birth: _____

Date of Death: _____

"There is no time or space that separates true love."

Kim Fehlhafer, grandmother of Cecelia

A Beautiful Hello

"I am forever blessed and made better by my beautiful granddaughter, who did not make a sound or do a deed. She just "was" in all of her divine love, innocence, and beauty. Knowing her changed me forever."

Kim Fehlhafer, grandmother of Cecilia

How You Embraced Life

Your Likes and Dislikes

_____

_____

_____

_____

_____

_____

_____

_____

"The death of a child is not natural. It defies the "natural order" of the universe. The un-naturalness of the child dying before the parents disrupts the proper scheme of things. The universe does not seem to be unfolding as it should. That shakes us up... profoundly. We are not the people we were and never will be."

Mindy Kankel, mother of Mari

A Heartbreaking Goodbye

_____

_____

_____

_____

_____

_____

_____

_____

Days are hard, and we get through them as best we can. I'm a mom consumed with sadness and emptiness without Sarah.

Julie Reiss, mother of Sarah

The Service We Held to Honor You

_____

_____

_____

_____

_____

_____

_____

_____

_____

_____

_____

_____

_____

_____

_____

_____

_____

_____

I have no idea what to do now, other than take it one day at a time and find comfort in knowing that we have the most amazing angel watching over us.

Shelby Schumacher, mother of Brody

Our Reflections of the Day

_____

_____

_____

_____

_____

_____

_____

_____

_____

_____

_____

_____

_____

_____

_____

_____

_____

_____

In the days shortly after Elliott's death, we felt as though time was standing still immediately in front of us. The world was continuing on around us, but through the halting feelings of grief, we felt an immense sense of love and support from our close family and friends, and God.

Sarah and Nick Ryan, parents of Elliott

Special People in Your Life

_____

_____

_____

_____

_____

_____

_____

_____

_____

_____

Thoughts About You From Your Family

Learning to Live Without You Here

_____

_____

_____

_____

_____

_____

_____

_____

Unbelievably (and unbearably), the rest of the world goes on.

Mindy Kankel, mother of Mari

Questions I Want to Ask You

_____

_____

_____

_____

_____

_____

_____

_____

_____

Missing You...

_____

_____

_____

_____

_____

_____

_____

_____

_____

_____

Times When It Is The Hardest

_____

_____

_____

_____

_____

_____

_____

_____

_____

_____

Grieving Shattered Dreams

_____

_____

_____

_____

_____

_____

_____

_____

I remember how disoriented I was....I couldn't figure out how to pay bills because I couldn't find my checkbook and when I found my checkbook, I forgot why I was looking for it. I didn't know how to even begin to pull a meal together for my family. It all just seemed too overwhelming.

Jeanie Kochan, mother of Avery

One thing Nick and I vowed was that as we went through the stages of grief so differently and often times at complete opposite ends of the spectrum of emotion, we would not let that pull us apart, but yet draw us closer, as we are bonded in the life and loss of Elliott, and that is something no one else has.

Sarah and Nick Ryan, parents of Elliott

Things We Do To Honor You

_____

_____

_____

_____

_____

_____

_____

_____

_____

I fervently wish to honor her and cherish her loving legacy to us by living a full, productive and happy life. I know that she would have wanted that for her family and friends.

Mindy Kankel, mother of Mari

Special Days We Remember You

_____

_____

_____

_____

_____

_____

_____

_____

_____

Special Days We Remember You

_____

_____

_____

_____

_____

_____

_____

_____

If she had not been such a beacon of light, life, love and hope, perhaps I wouldn't be so aware of the darkness.

Mindy Kankel, mother of Mari

Finding Our Way

_____

_____

_____

_____

_____

_____

_____

_____

As a family, we embrace each other, our faith, and our belief that Sarah is happy....and wants us to be happy, as well.

Julie Reiss, mother of Sarah

Reflections

_____

_____

_____

_____

_____

_____

_____

_____

Sure, we can talk about you without crying, but that comes with time. There are still nights when your mommy cries herself to sleep because there is a place in our hearts that you took with you; that place will never be filled again.

Shelby Schumacher, mother of Brody

Reflections

We want people to talk about Sarah, even if we cry. They're not reminding us that she died; they're reminding us that they remember her...that's a gift to us.

Julie Reiss, mother of Sarah

The Way Things Change...

_____

_____

_____

_____

_____

_____

_____

_____

_____

_____

Our Story...Woven Together

I would describe my love for Roshni--while she lived on earth--
as fierce. I wanted it to be this way always. But now, two years
later, I love her in a serene way, and this serenity, I've learned,
is okay. It allows me to live my life without the heavy burden of
grief and pain. Because I don't feel the pain, I sometimes wonder
if I've forgotten, and whether she is hurt or angered by this. I then
remind myself that she wants me to live in happiness and peace,
and that I don't need to lead a sorrowful life in order to give her the
special honor that she deserves.

Nalini Joseph, mother of Roshni